BAAA WARS

AN EWE HOPE

Derek the Weathersheep

"

Derek the Weathersheep's books have had me and my husband in stitches since 2012. They are unique, original and totally hilarious! If you're going to read one book this year, it has to be one of Derek's.

Amazon Review

DEDICATION

I'd like to dedicate this book to all those people who helped make the original and best sci-fi adventure of them all.

Derek the Weathersheep
Honey Farm
Brecon x

More books available at www.walesoncraic.com

BAAA WARS

CHAPTER ONE

It is a period of unrest in Wales. Almost all of the human race has been wiped out by man-flu (not even Lemsip could save them). Quick-thinking sheep have taken over the order of the earth. Lovely, fluffy White Sheep, striking from a hidden base in Tonyrefail, have won their first victory against the evil Black Sheep's Empire who run proceedings from the Senedd in Cardiff.

During the battle, White Sheep spies managed to steal plans for the Black Sheep's ultimate weapon - the Debt Star, a mobile debating chamber so powerful that it can legislate monthly wheelie bin collections without any due process or scrutiny.

Pursued by Black Sheep agents, Princess Dolly races home aboard her sheep transporter, custodian of the Black Sheep Empire's evil plans. With it, she hopes that the rebellion can restore bi-weekly wheelie bin collections and therefore freedom to the Universe.

CHAPTER TWO

On a road, just past the Little Chef outside Brecon, a sheep transporter made its way silently through the crisp winter's night.

It followed the path of the former A470, once the jewel of Western human civilisation; now nothing more than a smudge on the barren landscape. Gone were the 'catering' vans offering Pig's Bollocks and Eyeball Burgers in the lay-bys. Gone were the dickhead drivers in their Vauxhall Corsas who would pull out at Ponty without indicating. Gone were the doggers who'd park up at night and do whatever doggers do (rudey things like sniffing each others' bums I think). The road signs that once led the way to beautiful, tropical places like Aberdare and Treharris now hung broken and rusted. Things weren't the same now that sheep ruled earth. Nothing was like it used to be.

The sheep transporter wasn't a sheep transporter as you'd know it either. It had no wheels and didn't have an Ivor Williams Trailers sticker on the side. Oh no. This one was really sci-fi, like the sort of thing you'd see on Buck Rogers. That's because this story is set in the future. The transporter was about the size of a small motorhome and had a big sign on the side that read Tantric IV. It had no wheels but instead, it hovered about 3 feet off the ground and moved silently and slowly through the darkness. Its cargo was a very important ewe – Princess Dolly of Orgasma.

It had been a tiring day for Dolly. As an

important cog in the rebel machine, she had led the raid against the Senedd in the hunt for the secret Debt Star plans. And now that she had them in her possession, she was hoping to photocopy it at her secret hideaway and restore bi-weekly wheelie bin collections to the Universe.

Dolly's driver was an old, sad-looking sheep. He looked like he'd just found out that Honey G had released a Christmas single. Dolly was sat next to him on the front seat, her eyes clocking the speedometer and wishing that he would go a bit faster. And sat in between the two were her two furry dog companions, Arty-Farty and Sheepy-3-0. That's pronounced Sheep-Three-Oh by the way. Not Sheepy-Three-Zero because that would ruin the parody. The pair never saw eye to eye, mainly due to their difference in height.

The driver turned off the main road and onto a dark dirt track.

"This road is very dark, drive," said Dolly. "When was the last time they had any street lighting on here?"

"These roads are kept deliberately dark ma'am," replied the driver. "This is the road that rebel sheep used to ferry bootleg batches of Malted Milks to the farms back in the days of the human settlements. Not even the humans knew of these roads. Stocks of Malted Milks are dwindling and today's smugglers want to keep an even lower profile. I'm having to rely on experience to get through these roads."

The road was indeed dark. It was so dark, it was as if you had closed your eyes really, really tight and then put a blindfold on and shut the light off. Or as if you were blind. The only way you'd know if there was a sheep transporter passing through was if you stepped out into the road and got hit by it.

Suddenly a red light started flashing on the driver's dashboard.

"What is it?" asked Dolly anxiously.

"It's a flashing red light," replied the driver.

Behind the transporter, out of the gloom and darkness loomed a menacing huge spaceship, just a few feet off the ground. Its dark triangular shape edged closer to Dolly's transporter. It was a bit like that scene from Close Encounters - you know the one where he's sat in his car looking at his map and these lights just come up behind him and that. Aw. Great movie that one.

"Looks like we've got company," said the driver, pretending that he was in some kind of Hollywood blockbuster. He looked nervously in his rear view mirror. He'd seen a Black Sheep Destroyer before but not this close. His woolly arse began twitching with nerves.

Dolly wound down the window and looked back behind the Tantric. The destroyer following them was huge. It had lots of flashing lights on it and make a kind of rumbling sound, like the sort of sound a fully-laden Eddie Stobart truck would make as it passes down the High Street. Dolly immediately swung her head back inside the cab and picked up the CB that was attached to the dashboard. She squeezed the mouthpiece.

"You going to overtake? Over."

There came no reply. She tried again.

"There's plenty of road. Do you want to overtake?"

"I don't think they want to overtake," said Dolly's driver.

"What do you mean?" she asked.

"That ship's got Black Sheep Empire

markings on it."

Dolly thrust her head out of the window again and looked back. Her driver was right.

"Bollocks," she said. "Big hairy sheep bollocks."

"They must have known you were on board," said the driver.

"I'd better get rid of these plans," she said, rolling up the small piece of paper she had in her hand. She turned to the smaller of the two dogs sat next to her.

"Right. Arty. I know this wasn't what you signed up for but I need to stick this piece of paper up your arse. If the Black Sheep take me, I need you and Sheepy-3-0 to run away from here as fast as you can. These plans need to reach Tonyrefail, with or without me. You understand?"

The two dogs panted eagerly. Dogs are so stupid.

"You'll need to be quick," said the driver, "I think they're going to try and ram us off the road."

"Just keep driving," ordered Dolly, pulling back the curtain that was hung behind their seats. She peered into the back of the transporter. Sat in almost near darkness were her four body guards - all old sheep from the old Rebellion. None of them could shoot for shit. In fact, some of them played the parts of bad guys in the hit TV show, The A-Team back in the 80s.

"This may get rough," said Dolly. Her bodyguards pulled out their weapons and prepared them for firing.

The transporter suddenly lurched forward as the destroyer nudged into the Tantric.

"Hold on!" said the driver.

Within a few seconds, the Black Sheep

destroyer had run the Tantric into a lay-by that was once popular with motorists who needed to stop for a piss. The Tantric skidded to a shuddering halt. Then there was silence.

The four in the front cab looked at each other. They were very afraid. You could tell that by the warm smell that rose up from down below.

"Boys. I need your help right now," whispered Dolly to her two dogs. "I'm about to be taken off this ship but I need to get that message to Autobahn 'Len' Konami."

Arty-Farty barked.

"Arty says that he's got a bardy leg and can't walk anywhere," said Sheepy.

"Well that's too bad. It's important. It's a message that will bring about the end of the Senedd's plans for monthly wheelie bin collections. We are struggling as it is with bi-weekly collections. If the Empire gets its way, they'll be introducing monthly wheelie bin collections all over the UK and we'll all suffocate under tonnes of rubbish. Now bend over," replied Dolly.

Arty duly bent over and Dolly stuck the rolled up piece of paper as far up his arsehole as she could get it. Before Arty could even whimper, there was a loud crash from the back of the van. Dolly instantly clambered into the back of the transporter to be with her bodyguards.

"Bollocks to this," said Sheepy-3-0. "I'm getting out of here."

The two dogs opened the door and leapt from the Tantric, scampering off out into the darkness of the fields.

At the rear of the transporter, it didn't take long for the Great Orme Troopers to bash open Dolly's back doors. Oo-er. There was lots of peow-

peowing and puffs and smoke and things but Dolly's bodyguards held their fire and waited for the right moment. They were going to zap whoever walked in. But silence fell once again.

With the back doors ripped off and smoke blanketing them, the bodyguards could smell the cool fresh air of the Brecon countryside. A huge cloud of smoke slithered into the Tantric. The bodyguards' fingers quivered on their laser guns, waiting for the right moment to let rip.

But before they could do anything, into the back of the transporter stepped the great dark figure of Garth Vaper, sucking on his e-cigarette. Rasping and sounding like the phonecalls that Dolly used to get from a pervert who lived on the same farm, Vaper stood there like he was modelling for Freeman's catalogue. His big black woolly frame filled the doorway and on his head, he had a big black mask with a little hole to pop his e-cig into.

"Here," he said to his Orme Trooper. "Can you hold this for me please?" He handed the Orme Trooper his e-cigarette and wafted the smoke around so he could see into the back of the transporter.

"Ah. There you are Orgasma. Cornered at last," he rasped.

Dolly looked up at him with terror in her eyes. And also some mascara that she'd smudged earlier when climbing into the back of the transporter.

CHAPTER THREE

Stood outside the transporter on the road, Dolly stood handcuffed facing Lord Vaper. We're not sure what happened to her driver or her bodyguards. Bit of a plot-hole that one. Sorry.

"The Imperial Senedd will not sit still for this. When they've heard that you've attacked a diplomatic mission, they'll go ape shit," she protested.

"Oh shut it your Highness. You're talking out of your fat backside. You aren't on any diplomatic mission at all and we all know it," said Vaper, puffing on his raspberry vape.

"I don't know what you're talking about. I'm a member of the Imperial Senedd and I'm on a diplomatic mission to Aldershot."

Vaper laughed. "Aldershot? You really are talking bollocks now. You're part of the Rebel Army who are fighting for bi-weekly bin collections and you know it. Guards – get her on board our destroyer and place her in one of the cells. We will take her to the Debt Star where she will await termination or rescue, whichever comes first."

The Orme Troopers grabbed her by her ears and led her away squealing.

"She'll tell me where this secret base is where they're all hiding," said Vaper to his guards. "I'll not have anyone questioning the Empire's monthly wheelie bin collection policy. Phone the Senedd and tell them that the transporter has crashed, killing everyone on board. I can then deal with this so-called Princess myself and at my own leisure."

Just then, a senior Orme Trooper stepped up to Vaper. His face was emotionless. A bit like Andy Murray when he won Wimbledon.

"Sir. No plans have been found on board this transporter. Two dogs ran off while you were off having a fag but they left empty-handed too."

"Send a detachment of Orme Troopers after the dogs," replied Vaper. "She must have given the dogs the plans to the Debt Star. She must think I was born yesterday. Find those plans and bring them to me. See to it personally Commander. Nothing will stop me this time."

He then let out an evil cackle, followed by a cough, a hack and a splat as he spat out a luminous green snot goblin that landed on his shoe.

***

Meanwhile, out in the middle of the Welsh valleys, Arty-Farty and Sheepy-3-0 were lost. I told you dogs were stupid. They hadn't come across any other living soul for hours and they were getting hungry.

"We seem to be made to suffer," said Sheepy-3-0. "Not only are we Welsh but we've been given the role of skivvies in this book."

"Woof," replied Arty-Farty, mainly because he couldn't speak a word of English.

Sheepy-3-0 looked around. Up ahead lay an abandoned Cash Generator shop and some empty cans of Stella, no doubt left there from its long-lost human inhabitants.

"What a desolate place this is. This must be the place they call Bedlinog," said Sheepy. "I heard about this place once. Mother Theresa once visited and ended up fighting the owner of a pub. Not like her at all."

"Woof," said Arty-Farty.

"This place is home to the Dwarf People of Bedlinog – the leftovers of the human race. Rumour has it that they inbred so much that murder cases couldn't be solved because the entire village had the same DNA."

"Woof," said Arty-Farty.

"What mission? What are you talking about?"

"Woof," replied Arty-Farty again.

"Will you stop going on about this bloody mission. I know you've got a very important piece of paper stuck up your arse but can you just leave it? We need to find a Travelodge or something."

"Woof."

"Haven't been able to shit for days? Well that's not my problem."

Arty looked south and headed away from the Cash Generator, down towards the deserted town of Bedlinog.

"Fine. Bollocks to you then. You go that way. I'm going over here," shouted Sheepy. "Looks like there's a farm over here anyway. I'll be able to get myself some proper sausages to eat."

Sheepy-3-0 headed off in the opposite direction from Arty but before long, he was finding himself lost once again. He was getting worried. Then, there came a flashing light.

"Oh! What's that?" His ears pricked up. "It's either a Stagecoach bus or it's the rozzers." He stood up on his hind legs and waved his two front legs around, hoping to catch the attention of whoever it was.

"Over here! Help me!" he shouted.

Meanwhile, Arty-Farty was making his

way into Bedlinog town centre. Danger lurked all around. Beady eyes peered out at him and he was getting a little bit worried himself. Worse still, his bowels had made some movement and he was in desperate need of a dump. With the important plans wedged firmly up there, he'd have to wait until he got to Tonyrefail.

"Here, doggy doggy," came a voice. A hand popped out from behind a burnt-out Mondeo and held out a packet of Space Raiders. Arty couldn't resist. He was starving. More impressively, they were still 20p. So much for Brexit.

No sooner had he stuck his nose in the bag of crisps, he felt a sharp pain on the back of his head and he fell over on one side.

"These Tasers have come in handy haven't they butt?" said the first Dwarfman of Bedlinog.

"Aye," said the other. "Lovely."

The Dwarf People of Bedlinog picked up Arty and put him in the back of their Transit van. Then they hopped in and drove off.

When Arty awoke, he was in the middle of a car park. He looked around. There must have been about 30 or 40 sheep stood around, some bartering for the dogs that had been collected by the Dwarfmen, and some bringing more in on Transit vans. For a moment, Arty thought he was at Splott Market.

He was surrounded on all sides by other dogs. He looked at the one next to him.

"Woof," barked Arty.

"We're bound for Bak I Moon's takeaway down the road," said the dog next to him who could speak English, "and some are bound for the fields as workers." The old dog next to him had one of those faces that looked like it'd be used for catapult practice by his mother.

Through blurred vision, Arty could make out the shape of Sheep-3-0 approaching.

"Oh am I glad to see you!" cried Sheepy, patting Arty on the top of his head.

"Woof," said Arty, because that's all he could say, like I said before. Do you not listen?

They both heard two voices coming across the car park.

"What about those two?" said the one voice. Sheepy and Arty looked up to see Derek the Weathersheep and his uncle Owain. The pair were looking for dogs to buy. They were looking to buy Arty and Sheepy-3-0. It was just as well as the rest of the story involves them attempting to save the Universe from monthly wheelie bin collections. Isn't that a coincidence, reader?

***

Owain, Derek's uncle, had learned to drive a human tractor when he was just a lamb. As the human race died out, they left a legacy of farm tractors all over the UK. It was the sheep who commandeered them and taught themselves how to drive them.

Owain's tractor however, was looking a little worse for wear. He hadn't changed the tyres in 20 years because there were no Kwik Fits open any more. It was also in serious need of a valet. When he got back to his farm, Owain took the tractor straight to the farm's barn where he dropped off Derek and the two dogs.

"I want them cleaned up," he ordered. "They'll be working the farm this time tomorrow." Arty looked at Sheepy.

"Woof," he said.

"Looks like your message will never get to Autobahn Konami now," replied Sheepy.

***

Derek was a bit of a boring fart. As sheep went, he really had nothing going for him at all. He had spent much of his life on his Uncle Owain's farm, having not really known his own parents. They had left him when he was just a lamb, probably because he was just so boring.

"I'll never leave the farm," he'd moan and then skulk about the fields like some miserable twat. Uncle Owain would often clip him around his ear and tell him to man up. To console himself, Derek would lose himself in meteorological charts and forecast the weather. He often dreamt of becoming a great weather presenter like Sian Lloyd, Ruth Wignall or even the late Ian McCaskill. At lunch at the trough later that day, it was the same old story.

"Derek, if you don't stop whinging, I'm going to stop you watching reruns of One Man and His Dog. I hope you've cleaned those bloody dogs too," snapped Owain, dipping his head in the trough. "I need them to work the farm."

"But Uncle, life around here is so boring," retorted Derek. "If I didn't have the weather to forecast, I'd literally be sat around doing nothing. I'll do the dogs this afternoon, I promise."

Owain lifted his head, his sheepy lips wet with water. The heat of the midday sun was crisping the back of his neck. "You sound like your old man. He was a miserable twat too," he muttered. "Now get those two dogs cleaned up. I want them working on the farm by tomorrow morning."

Derek sighed and headed over to the barn where the two dogs sat waiting. It was another hot day down on the farm and the two dogs just sat there panting.

"Come on," said Derek, heading into the barn. The two dogs followed. Because they're stupid and they'll do whatever you tell them to do.

***

After 10 minutes, even the dogs were shit bored of Derek's whinging.

"My Uncle Owain. He never lets me do anything around here," moaned Derek as he washed a wet sponge over Arty-Farty's body. Arty loved being washed but it wasn't the relaxing bath he would have loved. He was on a mission. He had to get the message to Autobahn Konami.

"Woof," said Arty-Farty.

"He's trying to tell you something Master," Sheepy-3-0 piped.

Derek didn't want to listen. Instead, he wanted to tell the two dogs about how he was never allowed to play out in the fields after dark and how he never had any friends.

"I'd sometimes just look out at the fields from the barn and want to do something with my life; go somewhere, be someone..."

Before Derek could finish his boring sentence, he noticed the white piece of paper hanging out of Arty-Farty's arse.

"Hey. What's this hanging out of this dog's butthole?" Derek gently tugged at the piece of white paper that hung out of Arty-Farty's backside, but it failed to budge. He tried again.

"Just..need..to…" he said in quite a dramatic fashion to make it sound a bit more exciting than it actually was, but he pulled too hard and he was left holding a sliver of paper.

"Sigh. I can't even pull a piece of paper out of a dog's arse properly," whined Derek.

"Try again Master Derek," said Sheepy. Derek carefully pulled at the piece of paper and with one firm tug, he pulled another piece of paper clean out of Arty's arse. He unfurled it at arm's length and began to read it out loud for the reader's benefit.

"Help me Autobahn Konami. You're our only hope," he said. He turned to Sheepy-3-0. "Hey. There's only half a message here. Who wrote this? Who needs help? I'll help. There's frig all going on around here."

"It was written by a Princess on our last transporter. You wouldn't want to get involved there Master. She's asking for trouble," replied Sheepy.

"What kind of trouble?"

"She's pushing for these bi-weekly wheelie bin collections Master Derek."

"What? Really? Wow. How exciting! Can I get involved? We could really do with bi-weekly collections around here. The amount of rubbish that Owain puts out is horrendous and it only gets collected once a month. He spends half of his weekends fly-tipping in the village down the road. Where will I find this Princess?"

"Don't ask me," replied Sheepy. "The rest of the message is up Arty's arsehole."

Derek looked at the piece of paper that he held in his hand and read it again. "Wow. She has lovely handwriting for a sheep. Bet she's pretty hot too. I'd love to see her tied up in chains and dressed in a golden bikini. Maybe another time eh? Oh how exciting! I hope this turns into some crazy intergalactic adventure."

Derek didn't know how true those words were to become.

***

Down at the trough that evening, Derek was lapping up some feed with Uncle Owain.

"That dog had a piece of paper up its arse, Uncle. From a Princess apparently. Looking for Autobahn Konami. You don't think she's after that old cockwomble Len Konami from the mountains do you?"

"Dunno," replied Owain "You're best not getting involved."

"Hm. I wonder. I saw him once wandering around the ruins of Ponty, looking for empty Corona pop bottles," mused Derek, his eyes wandering up into the sky.

"Like I said," continued Owain, "best left alone."

Derek sighed before talking again.

"I've decided that I'd like to go to Sheep College next year. I've been working on this farm for far too long. I'm bored shitless."

"But Derek, your weather forecasts are invaluable to this farm. What would I do without you? How would I know if it's going to rain for instance?"

"I could teach you the basics."

"Nah. I'd like you to stay on one more year. You can go to Sheep College then. Without you, I wouldn't know what to do."

"What do **you** do on this farm, Uncle?"

"I don't know," replied Owain. "That's another plotline I can't explain away. But I need you."

Derek stood up, put his hooves on his hips and sighed.

"You're such a bellend, Uncle. It's no wonder my father never liked you," he said and trotted off up the field. He spent the rest of the afternoon getting pissed on Skol. Later that evening, as the sun went down, he went and stood at an outcrop overlooking the fields.

He was totally off his tits and as hard as he tried to look like some kind of hero, all he could do was try and focus his blurred eyes on the two suns he could see in front of him.

CHAPTER FOUR

Derek woke with a jolt. He looked up to see Sheepy-3-0 stood over him.

"I'm afraid Arty-Farty's done a runner," whimpered Sheepy. Derek jumped up immediately.

"The little shit. Owain's going to do his nut if he finds out. Quick! Come with me!"

Derek opened the barn door and scampered across the fields with Sheepy in hot pursuit.

After an hour or so, the pair found themselves lost in the mountains. Derek was getting scared. He'd heard all about the locals who used to roam these parts. They'd managed to survive the human wipeout by living off packets of gone-off Wagon Wheels. Rumour had it that some of them still lurked in the forests nearby.

From a nearby rock came the snap of a twig.

"Oh no," said Derek. "The sound of a twig snapping is usually a giveaway sign in a narrative form that there is danger close to hand." Before he could even think about what boring thing he was going to say next, a large boulder landed smack in his face and he fell to the ground like a sack of shit.

"Oh my!" gasped Sheepy. He turned to see three former residents of Treharris lurching towards him with cans of White Lightning in their hands. Sheepy knew these kind of humans existed but he'd never seen them in real life before.

"Wanna fight butt?" asked one. He was only two foot tall and had three eyes.

"What you looking at four eyes?" said another, which confused Sheepy a little as he wasn't wearing glasses.

The three lurched closer. Sheepy was rooted to the floor with fear. Derek was still sparko a few feet away. Sheepy looked like he was about to get himself involved in his first valleys fight.

Then, from out nowhere, there came a piercing bleat that bounded around the mountains and filled the ears of all those stood in this particular scene. The dwarf people of Treharris scarpered with their cans of White Lightning, leaving Sheepy even more scared than he was just a minute ago.

He looked up to see an old rugged ram with kind eyes moving towards him. Did that piercing bleat really come this old codger? The ram made his way down to Derek who lay motionless on the floor. The ram put his hands on Derek's forehead and muttered the words "Deus ex machina," and in an instant, Derek woke.

"Wow. How did you do that?" asked Sheepy.

"My name is Len. I can do magic. My middle names are Paul and Daniels. I was on Britain's Got Talent once. Got beaten by a dog. Bloody Simon Cowell."

Derek sat up and shook his head. "Len?" he asked.

"Yes. My name is Len. I can do magic. My middle names are Paul and Daniels. I was on Britain's Got Talent once. Got beaten by a dog. Bloody Simon Cowell. I've said that twice now and still no-one has said how impressed they are."

"We've been looking for you," said Derek "I've got a very important message to give to you."

"You'd better come back to my barn then," said Len.

***

Len's barn was a simple affair. A small smattering of hay on the floor led to what looked like an old mattress. And high on the wall hung a picture of Paul 'Paul' Daniels.

"You knew my father?" said Derek as he sat munching some grass that had been put in a bowl in front of him.

"Yes. He was a miserable twat. Always moping about the place feeling sorry for himself. We gave him everything we wanted but I think we spoiled him a bit too much. He was a lovely sheep growing up. And then he just…" Len stopped himself.

"What?" said Derek "He just what?"

Len chose his words carefully. "He just…it doesn't matter." He stood up and wandered over to the corner of his barn. He picked up a telescopic garden handle and handed it to Derek.

"Here. I have something for you." Len leant over and handed Derek the handle.

"What is it?" asked Derek in awe.

"It's a telescopic garden handle with no attachment on the end. You can attach various heads to it but you can also use it to poke people in the eye with it. It used to belong to your father."

"My father? What use would he have with a telescopic garden handle with no attachment on the end?"

Len sat down and sighed. "Your father was a Scabby Knight. When humans died out and us sheep took over, some lads decided to train themselves in the art of the Scabby. This weapon here was of great use to him, especially when the rise of the Black Sheep began. They came into our valley and tried to take our barns. Your father kept them at bay by poking them in the eye with this telescopic handle here."

Derek slowly rolled the telescopic handle over in his hooves. His eyes were full of awe.

"Wow," he said. "My eyes are full of awe."

"Your father was killed by Garth Vaper. He's a nasty piece of work. He's the loon who wants to implement these monthly wheelie bin collections."

Derek sat up straight. "Monthly wheelie bin collections?" he raged.

Len was taken aback by Derek's sudden anger. "Of course."

Derek was livid. "Monthly wheelie bin collections are out of the question. It's impossible; it's absurd. People will be struggling to get all their waste in their bins and we'll surely see the rise of fly-tip…"

"Stop!" cried Len, raising his hooves. "I know!" He lowered his tone. "I know. Now what's this message you speak of?"

Derek sighed. "It's up the dog's arse." He beckoned Arty-Farty over and pointed his arse to Len. "You'll have to get it out yourself. I got some of it out earlier."

Len leant forward and with a magic click of his Paul Daniels fingers, the rolled up piece of paper shot out of Arty's arse and landed on his lap. Carefully, Len unravelled it and read it to himself. He then looked up.

"We need to go to Aldershot," said Len solemnly.

"I can't go to Aldershot, Len. I've got my Uncle's farm to think about," quipped Derek.

"I'm afraid it's too late for them. Garth will have traced the dog to the farm. I presume he's been microchipped?"

Derek stood up. "I've got to go!" he bleated and dashed out of the barn into the daylight. He jumped on the tractor and turned the ignition.

"It's too late," called Len but Derek had started the engine and was halfway across the field.

CHAPTER FIVE

The tension in the Empire's meeting room was tighter than a duck's arse.

General Sweathead was putting forward his case to the room.

"I am worried. If the blueprints to this Debt Star are to fall into rebel hands, they could easily spot any weaknesses. All it takes is one banana in our exhaust pipe and it all goes tits up. That's a metaphor by the way."

"Have no fear," replied Grand Muff Larkin as he strode into the meeting room. "Anyone for a Malted Milk?" Grand Muff Larkin was a skinny man, despite his addiction to Malted Milk biscuits. It was the picture of the cows on them that did it for him. They reminded him of the good old days when humans farmed the animals of the world for their flesh, their skin and their fur. At least there was some comfort to be had in all that certainty.

There was a general mumble around the room but no takers for Muff Larkin's offer. The last person who took up his offer had his bollocks blown off so there was no rush to take any today.

"Good," continued Grand Muff. "You'll be pleased to know that something's just happened that I'm not quite sure about but it means that monthly wheelie bin collections will now be implemented across the whole Universe once this Debt Star is complete."

But Sweathead continued to plead his case:

"But there will be an outcry about these monthly collections. And as long as the Debt

Star is unfinished, the rebels have the potential to ruin it for us by posting about monthly wheelie bin collections on social media and causing an uprising. We need this Debt Star operational as soon as we can before we start shooting our mouths off about our capabilities."

"The Debt Star, even in its unfinished state is still the most powerful legislative room in the world," piped up General Fatty from the other side of the table. "The rebels would be fools to try and attack it."

"But we know that the rebels have those plans in their possession," protested General Sweathead.

There came a sudden coughing and spluttering and in a haze of pink smoke, Garth Vaper entered the room.

"Those plans will soon be back in our hands," he said reassuringly.

General Fatty started again:

"Our Debt Star can ruin entire communities, entire towns even. All we need to do is hover our beloved Debt Star over a town and legislate there and then. We could do it to any city in the UK right now. We don't need to wait for its completion. Come on lads. Let's give it a whirl eh?"

But Vaper was more cautious. He sucked on his e-cigarette long and hard before speaking.

"Don't be too rash," he said calmly. "The power to implement monthly wheelie bin collections for the sake of it is nothing compared to the power of the Morse."

"Don't talk bollocks Mr. Vaper," said General Fatty. "Your devotion to that load of arse is..."

But before he could get the rest of his sentence out, Vaper blew smoke into his face, and

Fatty struggled for breath.

"I find your lack of faith a little disturbing," said Vaper. Fatty continued to struggle for breath in a very dramatic fashion. His years at the Royal Welsh College of Music and Drama was finally paying off.

"Enough!" called Grand Muff. Vaper sighed like a stroppy teenager and went to sulk in the corner.

"Vaper will provide us with the location of the rebel hideout. Once we have done that, we will crush them by implementing monthly wheelie bin collections in one swift stroke. They will suffocate under black bins and food bags. They will regret ever taking us on."

***

Derek pulled up his tractor back at Uncle Owain's farm. Smoke billowed from the barn and the farm house was also on fire. He knew he was probably too late.

He turned off the ignition, pulled up the handbrake and set the alarm which make a kind 'wap-wap' noise. Then he started slowly for the house. He couldn't believe his eyes. There, lying in front of him was his uncle. And he was dead. Not pretend dead either. Proper dead. Like with his tongue lolling out of his mouth and his eyes all roly-poly and all that. Oh yes. He was very dead.

Alongside him was his auntie. She didn't look too healthy either but that was ok because she was always asking Derek to tidy his room and at least he wouldn't have to do that any more.

Derek stood up tall, looked to the sky and sighed. He wasn't sure why. He just thought it looked very dramatic. And lo, it was.

***

The next day, Vaper was in a really bad mood. He'd got up late and missed his usual three Weetabix. He wasn't very good in the mornings to be honest. He'd press snooze on his alarm until even his phone gave up trying to get him out of bed. When he did finally get out, he'd be utterly useless without a cup of coffee. And even then, if he didn't have his Weetabix, he'd punch someone in the face for just looking at him. That's how nasty he was.

This particular morning, he was in a grump as he still hadn't located the plans that had been stolen by the rebels. He grabbed a guard and headed down to the cell where Dolly was being held captive. Once he was there, he got the guard to open the door. That's how bossy he was.

"You will tell me where your secret base is," he rasped. He pushed his big black sheepy nose into Dolly's face. His breath stank. Like a hippo's breath.

"No I won't," replied Dolly. She'd only just woken up too and her makeup was all over the place.

"Yes you will."

"No I won't."

"Yes you will."

"No I won't."

"Hm. Playing hardball are you? I see. We'll play it your way then. Guard. Fetch me the Justin Bieber CD."

The guard stood motionless before he started to stammer. "But, but but..."

"Just get it!" barked Vaper. The guard dashed

out of the room while Vaper leant into Dolly's face. "Now we'll get you talking."

CHAPTER SIX

Len could tell that Derek had been crying when he returned. His eyes were all red and the fleece around his eyeballs were all wet and sticky. Len knew what had happened.

"Chin up, eh lad?" said Len.

"I'm coming with you," croaked Derek as he approached Len.

"To Aldershot?"

"Yes."

"Have you made a packed lunch?"

"No. I'll get something at the services. I think they do a meal deal. A sandwich, a packet of crisps and a bottle of Fanta for £20. I know it's expensive but I don't have anything on me right now."

"Fine. We'll head to Aust spaceport and find someone who's going to Aldershot. Let's go," explained Len.

***

Aust spaceport was crawling with spaceships, aliens and other things that I can't be bothered to describe right now. The remnants of Severn View Service Station, once famed for having the cleanest toilets of any service station in the UK, was now overrun by all kinds of creatures. No AA salesmen here. No people trying to sell you credit cards and definitely no massage chairs. Those days were long gone. Aust was now an intergalactic hub where creatures from all over the Universe arrived and left. It was a bit like Newport bus station but with nicer toilets.

Derek, Len, Arty and Sheepy made their way into the main drag of this small, sandy city. They watched as a large spaceship swung in low over them and landed at an empty bay just ahead of them.

"This looks like fun," said Derek. "I only said earlier that I hoped I'd find some adventure. And here we are, not too far from Chepstow. Where else would you find such adventure?"

"Stop right there!" came a booming voice from behind. The four turned around to see three Orme Troopers pointing pointy sticks at them.

"Where are your papers?" said one. Derek gulped. He knew that they didn't have any papers and if they were rumbled, the Orme Troopers would not hesitate to turn him and Len in to Garth Vaper.

Len lifted his Paul Daniels fingers and gave them a little wiggle like he was sprinkling a dash of pepper on his pizza. Except he never ate pizza because he was a sheep.

Derek watched in amazement as the Orme Troopers simply waved them on their way.

"Wow," said Derek. "You really are like Paul Daniels aren't you?"

Len chuckled. "Yes. Yes I am. But without a Debbie McGee to speak of," he replied. He was a wise sheep indeed.

They approached a Wetherspoons pub, once the haunt of the humans who used to live there. Len tied the two dogs to a post outside with a bit of string that he just happened to have and he then led Derek in through the door into the pub.

Len walked up to the bar.

"Are you wanting me to do a joke at this point?" said the barman.

"No," said Len. "I'll just have two Skols please. And I need to know if you know anyone who'll take me to Aldershot." The barman poured two beers and pointed to a sheep who was sat in one of the cubicles. Sat alongside him was a 7ft tall llama.

"He's your man. The one there with the llama. He goes to Aldershot all the time."

Len thanked the barman, took the two beers and approached the sheep and llama in the cubicle.

"May we join you?" he asked.

"Sure," said the sheep sitting up in his seat. The llama made a funny llama sound because that's what llamas do when they're trying to say hello.

"I understand you may be able to get us to Aldershot," asked Len. "My name's Len and this here is Derek." Len introduced Derek to the sheep.

"My name's Juan Iolo," said the sheep. "I'm half-Spanish, half Welsh, half Canadian. This here is Chico. He's a llama and he comes with me everywhere."

"Nice," acknowledged Len. "Can you get us safe passage to Aldershot? I've already asked you once and you just ignored me."

"Depends how much you're paying."

Len patted his sides. "I can sort you out with a score. We are in a bit of a hurry. We can't get stopped by any of the Dark Side though. Will your ship get us there quickly?"

"I own the Millennium Pigeon," boasted Juan, taking a swig of his Skol and wiping his mouth with the back of his wrist.

"What's that?" asked Derek.

"Have you never heard of the Millennium Pigeon?"

"No. Why? Should I have?"

Juan sat back in his seat with a proud smirk across his face.

"The Millennium Pigeon is the ship that made the kessel run in less than 12 parsecs."

Len looked confused. "You do realise that a parsec is a measurement of length and not of time don't you? What you've just said is literally a load of old bollocks."

"Erm…yeah," said Juan, sipping his drink quickly.

"I'll give you £10 cash now and I'll get some money out of the cash machine at Aldershot and give you another tenner," said Len. "No questions asked."

"Deal," said Juan. "Meet in Bay 94. Chico, go and get the ship ready. The toilet might need cleaning as I was in a rush when I left this morning."

Derek and Len stood up and quickly left, followed by Chico. Juan was about to follow when he was stopped by a freaky-looking thing who pointed a water pistol in his face.

"Ah. Greedy. I was just looking for you," said Juan, slinking back into his seat.

The green-looking alien started talking gibberish. He was clearly vexed about something.

"I was just about to go to the cash point and get some money for you," said Juan. "If you follow me, I'll go get it." Juan and Greedy stood at the same time, both heading for the door.

"You go first," said Juan, offering Greedy the way.

Greedy spoke more alien bollocks.

"No. Please. You go first."

This argument went on for a bit until they both started walking out at exactly the same time to avoid making Juan look like some kind of ruthless cad before his character had fully been fleshed out in the narrative.

***

Up in the sky, aboard the Debt Star, Princess Dolly was still tight-lipped about the whereabouts of the Rebel Base. And Garth Vaper was getting increasingly frustrated.

"She's still not talking," he said "I've even played the Justin Bieber album. With bonus track. Twice. She's tougher than we thought."

Grand Muff Larkin wasn't impressed either. He stroked his woolly black face, his yellow eyes staring out of the window.

"Then she leaves us no choice," he said finally. "We shall have to make Aldershot a monthly-bin collection zone with no delay."

Garth spluttered on his e-cigarette. "We can't do that, mun. It's not even in Wales."

Grand Muff Larkin turned to Garth. "You really do underestimate the power of the Debt Star, Lord Vaper. We can do anything we want. This is sci-fi after all. There are no rules."

Garth sucked in hard on his vape. He sucked so hard that his mouth went all tight and wrinkly like a tiny pink little anus. Then he bellowed out a huge amount of smoke and steam.

"Oo, you are naughty Larkin," he said, giggling.

***

Juan Iolo came belting down the main strip of Aust. His stumpy little sheep legs moved so fast, they all became a furry blur. Behind him followed several Orme Troopers, all guns blazing, the zappers kicking up dust around Iolo's trotters. Juan knew that Bay 94 wasn't far but he had to shrug off his pursuers. He'd shot the green alien thing in the face as soon as he was out of the pub and the Orme Troopers were now giving chase.

He rounded the bend to Bay 94 and ducked inside the doorway. The Millennium Pigeon was there waiting for him along with Len, Derek, Arty, Sheepy and Chico, who was kicking the ship's tyres.

"Quick!" yelled Juan. "We got to go!" He raced straight up the gantry and boarded the ship, the rest of the entourage following him swiftly because they didn't want to be shot in the arse.

Juan leapt into the driver's seat and put his seatbelt on. "Close the doors! Start the engines! Put Classic FM on! Wind down the windows!" The hum of the engines stirred and within seconds, the ship rose slowly into the air like some sort giant spaceship.

Peow peow peow!

The Orme Troopers burst into Bay 94 and started blasting their guns all over the place. Juan slammed the throttle forward and with one almighty blast, the Pigeon roared off into the sky. It took a few minutes for the team to catch their breath. Out of the window down below, Derek could see the fields and the Bristol Channel passing beneath them.

"Ok. We've got to get this ship into hyperspeed," muttered Juan. He ran his trotters over a line of switches and pulled on a few levers. There came a sudden crash from behind and the ship shuddered with the explosion. Juan looked in his rear view mirror.

41

"Looks like we've got company," he said. "Chico. Take the controls. I've got to fight them off."

Juan unbuckled his seatbelt, jumped up and headed down the galley towards the gun deck that hung underneath the ship like a big pair of bollocks.

He strapped himself in to the seat and looked out. Two Clark's Pie Fighters were doubling back and heading for the Pigeon. Juan trained his crosshair on the nearest fighter and waited till he could see the whites of their eyes (it's a technical term that shouldn't be taken too literally as the baddies were wearing helmets).

The Clark's Pie fighter came screaming in, shooting his guns like no-one's business. All the fighter's shots missed but Juan held his nerve, his finger twitching on the trigger.

Peow! Peow!

Juan let rip with a volley of shots that plunged straight into the Pie Fighter, ripping off one of its wings and sending it into a dramatic spin. As it disappeared out of view, Juan heard the definite thud as the one Pie Fighter crashed into the second. The resulting explosion rocked the ship but Juan knew he had just taken out two enemies with one hit. He looked at his radar. Sure enough, the screen was empty.

"Bingo," he muttered to himself.

***

Princess Dolly stood with tears in her eyes as Vaper stood over her. In the corner of the room, Grand Muff Larkin was sat sticking pins in a Hillary Clinton doll.

"You let us down Princess. Worse than that

– you downright lied to us. There was no rebel base in Aldershot. I'm not happy." Vaper was not in a very good mood at all. Again.

"Alright. Alright," Dolly cried. Her voice quivered. "I'll tell you as long as you promise not to harm anyone."

Garth Vaper leant into her once again.

"Come on. I'm not all bad," he croaked.

"Yes you are."

"Bollocks. I gave money to Children In Need one year. NOW TELL ME WHERE THE REBEL BASE IS SO I CAN GET THESE BLOODY PLANS BACK BEFORE THEY PHOTOCOPY THEM!"

Dolly started to whimper.

"TELL MEEEEEEEEEEEEE!" raged Vaper.

"Aberystwyth," she stuttered. "You'll find the plans in Aberystwyth. Down by the library." Grand Muff Larkin's face cracked as his old crusty face smiled. He put his Hillary Clinton doll down and paced over to Dolly.

"Good girl. That's all you had to say," he said. "And to thank you for that, I'd like you to be the first to witness the power of the Debt Star. Take a look there. What do you see?" He pointed to a big screen that they'd managed to loot from an old Curry's store. On the screen was an image of Aldershot taken from an on-board camera.

"Larkin, you leave Aldershot alone. The people there are lovely. It's got a top quality Greggs and…"

"Guards! Give Aldershot monthly wheelie bin collections at your discretion," he sneered.

"NOOOOOOOO!" called Dolly.

"And after this, send her back down to the cell. We'll deal with her later."

Dolly couldn't tear her eyes away from the

screen as the refuse lorries in Aldershot went back to their yard to park up for a month.

***

Aboard the Pigeon, the commotion of the Clark's Pie Fighters had long been forgotten as they continued their merry journey to Aldershot. Derek had been practising swinging his telescopic garden handle around and poking things when Len suddenly felt a twinge in his gut.

"You ok Len?" asked Derek, dropping his stick.

"No," replied Len, clutching his belly. "Something terrible has just happened."

"Have you let one off?" asked Derek.

"I'm not quite sure. You get to a certain age and you never can tell."

Then, without warning, Chico slammed his mobile phone down on the desk in front of him.

"Whatever's the matter with him, Master Juan?" asked Sheepy.

"Angry Birds. He's been stuck on Level 29 for weeks," said Juan.

"Shall I show him how it's done?" asked Sheepy.

"Nah. He'll probably get mad and rip your head out of its socket," sniggered Juan. Things were getting jittery aboard the Millennium Pigeon.

Derek picked up his telescopic garden handle and began swinging it round wildly again.

From his pocket, Len picked out a tennis ball that he just happened to have on him. He had pockets like Sport Billy. He tossed it at Derek, hoping that he would bat it away but Derek didn't see it and it just twatted him in the face.

"You need to use the Morse," said Len.

"What the frig are you on about with this Morse rubbish?" replied Derek.

"You're trying too hard. Go with your instinct. I'll throw you the ball again and you need to bat it away but don't try too hard. Just let it flow. Like you would when you're busting for a piss. Try too hard and it doesn't come. Just relax."

Len picked up the ball and threw it at Derek again. This time, Derek swung and caught the ball cleanly. It shot over the other side of the room and out of sight.

"See?" said Len. "You've taken your first step towards becoming an intergalactic hero of sorts."

Just then, an alarm started sounding and it roused Juan from his comfortable seat where he'd been watching some EweTube videos.

"Looks like we're coming up on Aldershot," he said and headed for the cockpit. Chico followed, as did Len and Derek.

Once there, the group peered out of the window.

"Where's Aldershot?" asked Derek.

"There ain't no Aldershot," replied Juan, pulling the throttle back and swinging the Pigeon in low over a huge mound of rubbish. He peered longer out of the window, hoping to make out some sort of civilisation. But there was nothing.

"It looks like monthly bin collections have already started here," said Len. He was always the wise one. A bit like Gandalf but with a less impressive beard and a scruffier outfit. "They've been buried under their own rubbish. Aldershot is no more."

"Let's get out of here before we get noticed," said Juan, pushing forward on the throttle.

But they had been noticed. The Pigeon's engines strained but the ship refused to move. Confused, Juan looked at his dashboard, then the radar. There on the screen was a big blob.

"It's a planet," said Len.

"That ain't no planet, dickhead. It's a battle station and they're pulling us in," yelled Juan.

"It's the Debt Star," muttered Len.

"That's not good is it?" asked Derek.

"No. Not good at all."

CHAPTER SEVEN

Garth Vaper sat back in his favourite chair and took in a huge toke of his e-cig. There was nothing he liked more than inhaling a lungful of unregulated chemicals and nicotine to make him feel better.

His office aboard the Debt Star was a simple yet elaborate affair. The walls were bare, painted in Airfix grey. One wall was devoted entirely to his assortment of e-cigarettes and liquids. All his flavours were arranged by category and in alphabetical order: beverage, candy, cereal, coffee, cream, custard, dessert, fruity, menthol, milk, nut, sweet and tobacco. He even had a wide selection of vape tanks and an endless supply of batteries. On another wall, he had a large flat-screen television where he could watch his favourite TV shows and in the middle of the room was his large desk and his comfortable chair. On his desk was a framed picture of himself.

There came a knock at his door.

"Come." The door opened and one of his generals popped his head around.

"Sorry sir. We've just picked up a freighter that was on its way to Aldershot. It left Aust Spaceport earlier this afternoon. We believe it was carrying two dogs. Would you like us to search it?"

"Yes captain. And once you've found them, set course for the Senedd," said Vaper "And close the door on your way out."

"Aye, aye sir." The general left the room. Vaper lifted the TV remote control and paused the episode of Going For Gold he'd been watching so that he could talk to himself in a sinister manner. He gently tapped his fingertips together and smiled an evil smile. Which was about as useful as that second shift key on a keyboard because he was wearing a mask and no-one could see his evil smile.

"If those plans are aboard that ship, we can crush the Rebellion once and for all," he said.

***

The Millennium Pigeon sat in the hangar of the Debt Star. Despite Juan's best efforts, the tractor beams had been too strong and had pulled them in. There was nothing he could do.

Orme Troopers buzzed about the docked ship, blasters in their hands. They were waiting for orders to board and search the Millennium Pigeon. Garth Vaper strutted into the hangar and immediately started dishing out orders like a big bossy baddie.

"Go aboard and search every square inch. I want those plans found. If you find anyone, bring them to me personally."

"Yes m'Lord," said the Orme Trooper and led a small group of them on board. But like an incompetent husband who'd been sent to look for his wife's bra in the ironing basket, they didn't look very hard and stepped back off the ship to report that they'd found nothing. On board, Juan, Derek and the two dogs popped up from underneath some dodgy flooring where they had been hiding.

"Phew. That was a lucky escape," said Derek. "I'm so glad those Orme Troopers can't see very well. It's no wonder their shooting isn't up to scratch."

"Yes," said Juan, "Now come on. We need a

plan to get out of here." He pulled himself out of the floor and dusted himself down.

"Woof," barked Arty.

"Yes, you're' right," nodded Sheepy.

"What did he say?" asked Derek.

"He says that at this point in time, it looks like we have no way of getting off this ship. Worse still, the guards have said that they will conduct a thorough search which means that should we stay on board, we are surely to be found. We can't leave on the ship as we'll still be under the tractor beam so the only way out is to somehow shut down the tractor beam, reboard our ship and get out of here. Added to that, we also have the added pressure of locating the kidnapped Princess who may be aboard this battlestation, and rescue her if applicable. It seems an impossible task right now so here's what we'll do: we'll entice the Orme Troopers aboard the Pigeon somehow, twat them over the head, steal their uniforms and infiltrate the ship."

"Well done Arty," said Derek. "That sounds like a grand plan."

Juan peeped down the gangway. There were two Orme Troopers standing guard.

"Coo-ey!" called Juan. The two guards looked at each other before heading up the gangway. To cut a long story short, there was a bit of a Chuckle Brothers moment with some crashing and banging going on and a few minutes later, Juan stepped off the Pigeon dressed as an Orme Trooper. So far, so good.

Derek followed, also dressed as an Orme Trooper. Behind him came Len, Chico, Arty and Sheep-3-0, not dressed as Orme Troopers.

"The control room is up there," called Juan, leading the boys to an armoured door at the end of a corridor. They arrived at the door and knocked gently.

"Who is it?" came a voice from inside.

"Room service."

"Ah good," came the voice. "I'm bloody starving, me." The guard inside opened the door but as soon as he had, he realised his mistake. Before he could close it again, Chico had swiped one of his long muscular llama legs and taken the guard out. The guard slumped to the floor unconscious.

"Stop all this shooting! What is it with all these guns and that?" cried Derek, taking off his Orme Trooper helmet. Juan took his helmet off and couldn't wait to retort:

"If you want to save the Princess, you're going to have to shoot something," he snapped.

"Woof," barked Arty.

"Sir - Arty says that the piece of paper he had stuck up his arse will show you where the controls to the tractor beam are," said Sheepy.

Len took the paper out from his pocket and laid it on the desk in front of him before studying them carefully.

"Yes. I can see. If I can take one of these terminals, I should be able to take out the beam that's holding the ship here and we'll be able to get away."

Len thought in silence for a minute before looking up.

"There's not much you lads can do," he said "I'll need to go alone."

"But I want to come with you Len. You're an old sheep - you don't even know if you've farted or not. How are you going to make it out alive?"

"I'll use my Morse. It will be with you too. Always and forever. Amen."

And with that, Len slipped back out of the door and down the corridor. Derek closed the door behind him.

Juan turned to Derek.

"Where did you find that old codger? The cockwomble never even offered me a Werther's Original," he said.

"Len is a very wise old sheep," said Derek. He didn't like Juan talking about Len like that.

"Well. He needs to get some new incontinence pants, that's for sure."

Derek was about to kick off big time but Arty barked.

"What is it Arty?"

"He says that Princess Orgasma is here," Sheepy-3-0 piped up.

"The Princess? Here? Where?"

"Woof," said Arty.

"He says she's being kept in a cell down at the Detention Block, Cell Block H. She's being forced to listen to Justin Bieber around the clock."

"That's awful," said Derek.

"Yes. That's a bit below the belt," added Juan. "I've heard of some of the things the Empire has done to people but this is a new low."

"We need to rescue her," said Derek. He looked worried. His woolly brow pressed down over his eyes.

"I'm not going anywhere," said Juan. "The old gripper told us to stay right here." He put his feet up on the desk and relaxed back into his chair.

"But she's a Princess," said Derek.

"So?"

"She's got a big castle and stuff."

"So?"

"She's got loads of money."

"So?"

"She's got funbags the size of Zeppelins."

"Let's go," said Juan.

***

Len had managed to sneak down towards the power terminal but was farting around hiding behind pillars and generally being quite sneaky. He soon snuck up on Garth Vaper who was walking down a corridor puffing on his e-cig. He took one deep breath in but then stopped. He could sense that someone was there watching him. He'd had this feeling once before when he was showering in the gym.

Slowly, he peered over his shoulder and cast his eyes around the corridor.

Nothing. (There was really, but Len was hiding very sneakily behind a pillar). Vaper returned to his e-cig and then continued on his way.

***

Derek and Juan arrived at the Detention Block with Chico handcuffed between them. They had a very cunning plan and it involved Chico and some handcuffs, as you may have gathered. A guard stepped forward. He didn't look particularly friendly. A bit like the kind of guard you'd get at Passport Control.

"Who are you and how did you get in here?"

"I'm a locksmith and I'm a locksmith," chimed Juan.

"Hm. I've heard that gag before somewhere and it doesn't quite fit in here somehow," replied the guard. "Where are you taking this llama creature?"

"We're running a prisoner transfer," said Derek, ever the sensible one.

"Hm. I'll need to check on that. No-one's informed me. I'll just..."

Before the guard could say anything else, Juan had unloaded his blaster, knocking the guard clean off his feet and sending him sprawled all over the floor.

"I'll find out where the Princess is located. Derek - you go get her," yelped Juan, taking off his helmet so he could see what he was doing. Juan looked at the screen and prodded a few buttons as Derek dashed off up the tunnel towards the cells.

"She's in Cell Block H!" called Juan.

Just then, a voice come over the intercom.

"Everything ok lads?" said the voice.

"Erm. Yeah," said Juan. "You?"

"Who is this?" demanded the voice.

Juan had no answer. Instead, he took out his blaster and pumped a few lasers into it. The intercom fell silent.

"You're going to have to hurry Derek. They're on to us!"

Up the tunnel, Derek was faffing around looking for the right cell. Eventually, he found what he was looking for and opened the door. There, lying as if she was modelling for scattercushions, was Dolly.

"You're a little bit of a short arse for an Orme Trooper aren't you?" she said, a bit bemused.

Derek laughed, taking off his Orme Trooper helmet. "Oh, you are so funny," he said, tucking the helmet under his arm.

"Think I preferred you with the helmet back on actually," muttered Dolly.

"I'm Derek Fieldwalker and I'm here to get you out of here. I'm with Len Konami."

"Len Konami's here??" bellowed Dolly. "Well why didn't you say so?"

"I just did!" said Derek sheepishly.

"Let's go!" Dolly leapt to her feet and dashed out of the cell with Derek in hot(ish) pursuit.

CHAPTER EIGHT

Garth Vaper was worried. You couldn't really tell because he was wearing a big black mask so you'll have to take my word for it.

"Len Konami is here," he announced to the small gathering of generals sat in the meeting room.

Grand Muff Larkin looked around the room. "Where?"

"He's here. On the Debt Star."

"How can you be so sure?" chipped Muff Larkin. He wasn't in the mood for this touchy-feely stuff.

"I felt his presence."

"So you know what he's having for Christmas then?"

"Eh?"

"Don't worry. Old joke."

"Eh?"

Grand Muff stood up. "I said don't worry. It was an old joke."

Larkin's intercom buzzed and he stepped over to speak into it. "Yes? What is it?"

"Someone's kicked off down at the Detention Block, sir."

Muff clicked off the intercom and turned to Vaper.

"Maybe you're right."

"I am right. I told you so."

"Shut down all escape routes," ordered Muff Larkin.

"Konami won't be wanting to escape. I need

to face him alone," said Vaper.

And with that, Vaper turned on his heels, flounced his cape around like a big pansy and trotted out of the room.

***

Back at the Detention Centre, things were looking bad for Derek, Juan and the Princess. Orme Troopers had blasted their way into the control room forcing the trio back up the tunnel towards the Princess' cell.

Dodging laser blasts, Derek tried calling Sheepy-3-0 on his radio.

"Sheepy. Are there any other escape routes out of here? We're trapped!"

"Sir! There are Orme Trooper at our door. They're shooting their big zapper things. We're...."

Derek looked at his radio. It had gone dead. It seemed as if there was no way out. Again. Sigh.

"Bollocks," said Derek as a laser blast zipped past his furry head.

"Give me that," said Dolly, wrestling Derek's blaster from him. She took aim at a panel in the wall and fired. The panel flew off, leaving a gaping hole in the wall.

"Quick! Get in there!" she exclaimed.

"But that's the shitter," cried Juan.

"You got any better ideas?" she said and jumped into the hole. Chico and his long gangly llama legs followed while Derek and Juan tried to hold off the Orme Troopers.

"Get in there!" shouted Juan and Derek promptly jumped and disappeared down the hole. Juan made one last salvo at the Orme Troopers until he too, dived in, making the kind of noise a kid would make as they came down the water slide at Bluestone Holiday Park.

When he landed, he found himself up to his eyeballs in a water-filled room, full of floating turds and overturned Kwik Save trollies.

"Great. That last thing I wanted was to end up in Maesteg."

"Smells like Port Talbot in here, mun," muttered Derek, wafting his nose.

"We need to find a way out," said Dolly, wading around.

"Durr. Well said," smirked Juan. He was beginning to like this girl though he wasn't sure why. It must have been her funbags.

"There is no way out," said Derek. "Blimey. We really are finding ourselves in the most impossible scenarios recently aren't we? If we had Facebook accounts, we'd be all over this."

There was a plop in the water and the four of them looked around nervously.

"What was that?" asked Derek.

"I don't know," said Juan "but I don't like the sound of it."

Without any warning, Derek was dragged under the water like something from a 70s movie about a giant shark.

"Derek!" called Dolly. Derek burst to the surface, gasping for air.

"It's got me. Shoot it!!" he cried, before disappearing back under the water again. Juan fired off a few rounds of his blaster rather pointlessly and the room fell silent.

Dolly, Juan and Chico waited for Derek to appear. They waited. And waited.

And then Derek appeared, splashing around like some fish that had just been landed on a boat.

"What happened?" asked Juan.

"I dunno. Whatever it was just left me alone. I guess it didn't want to kill off the main character of the story halfway through the book."

"So all that was a bit pointless and dramatic?" said Dolly.

"Yes. Sorry about that."

A loud clunk shuddered the room and once again, the foursome were in trouble as the walls of the waste room began closing in on them.

Derek called frantically to Sheepy-3-0.

"Sheepy! Help us! Get Arty to turn off all the waste compactors!" which he did and they got out and that was that.

***

The Debt Star was now nearing the Senedd. But in one of the corridors, Len Konami was still sneaking around the place on tippy-toes. He was still looking for the terminal to shut down that would allow the Millennium Pigeon to escape. He opened a door and crept in through it. The pathway led to a platform, high in the air. On his tippy-toes, he made his way gingerly to the edge of the platform, where a control panel sat. He looked around to check that no-one was looking and then pulled on one of the levers. He watched as the counter showed the power of the tractor beam decrease to zero. Then he pushed a few more buttons for effect and snuck back out in the corridor.

Suddenly two Orme Troopers came around the corner. Len had no choice but to wiggle his Paul Daniels fingers and the pair's attention was diverted away from him so he could make his escape on tippy toes. What would he do without those magic fingers eh?

The tractor beam was down. All they needed to do now was to get back to the Pigeon and get the hell out of there.

***

Derek, Juan, Dolly and Chico arrived at a platform overlooking the hangar where the Millennium Pigeon was parked up. The Pigeon looked ready for flight but the hangar was not a safe place.

Derek clicked on his radio.

"Sheepy. Are you there?" he called.

Sheepy's voice crackled back over the radio.

"We're down at the hangar waiting for you."

"Great. We'll be down there now."

Derek turned to his friends. "Come on. We need to get to the ship so we can get out of here."

He dashed down another corridor and they followed. But as they rounded a corner, they ran straight into a billion Orme Troopers. Ok, maybe not a billion. But there was a lot of them. By lots, I mean a fair few. Not loads. Maybe ten or so.

"BLAST THEM!" ordered the lead Trooper.

Peow! Peow!

Both sides let off wave after wave of lasers.

Peow! Peow! All of the blasts missed everybody but the shock of seeing so many Orme Troopers sent Derek and his friends hurtling back down another corridor.

"They're going to get us!" cried Dolly.

"No they won't. We've got lots more books to feature in yet!" called Juan. "You go this way - I'm going to see if I can head them off at the pass!"

Derek and Dolly sprinted down yet another

corridor while Juan and Chico attempted to distract the Orme Troopers by heading back up and around to the hangar.

"Quick! In here!" called Derek, grabbing Dolly and pulling her behind a door. With a quick swipe, he closed the door behind them before realising they were stood on a ledge overlooking a chasm with no obvious means of escape. Across the other side of the chasm was an exit but it was too far for them to jump.

"Oh no," said Dolly. "We have no obvious means of escape and before long, a load of Orme Troopers are going to start shooting at us to add to the drama."

"Fear not," replied Derek. "If they carry on shooting the way they have been, we could spend all day here and not get hit."

Derek reached into his pocket and pulled out a tennis ball before realising that it was not useful and threw it down the chasm. Sure enough, a blast from the other side of the chasm skimmed his head and exploded behind them.

"What I need is some kind of hook on a rope," he said desperately, plunging his hand back into his pocket.

"Oh. Look. I've got one. Here, take this." Derek handed Dolly his blaster and swung the hook on a rope around his head like he was about to lasoo a cow. He was there for what seemed an age, tongue out the side of his mouth, taking aim.

"You going to be there all day doing that?" asked Dolly. She was running out of patience. Derek eventually launched his hook and by sheer fortune, it wrapped its way around a bit of metal and held firm.

"Here. Hang on to my love truncheon. I'm

going to do a Tarzan impression."

He grabbed Dolly and she grabbed his love truncheon and together they swept across the deep chasm to triumphant music.

***

Len was still lingering around the corridors of the Debt Star like a bad fart. In truth, he was biding his time. He knew he wouldn't be leaving on the Pigeon, but he wanted to make sure that the others could get away.

As he turned into a clearing, the dark looking figure of Garth Vaper was stood there, puffing on his e-cig.

"I've been expecting you," he said, his face shrouded in smoke.

"Doing Bond villain impressions now are you Vaper?" replied Len.

"When I last saw you, I was no more than a boy, in the company of strangers, in the quiet of a railway station..."

"Yes, yes, yes," yapped Len. "I get the picture. You're nothing but a big bully now though."

Garth pulled out his telescopic garden handle and Len did the same. It was going to be a fight to the death.

Garth launched first but Len was quick to react and blocked Garth's attack. Len then swung his telescopic garden handle up and over, looking to swing it down on Vaper's head but Vaper was wise to it and swung up to block the shot.

"You shouldn't have come back," said Vaper.

"I know. I could be sat at home watching Songs of Praise right now," replied Len, blocking another crushing blow from Vaper. Len slithered his telescopic garden handle and whipped it up from beneath's Vaper's chin, knocking his e-cig from his mouth and sending it spinning across the shiny floor.

"Oh, you've done it now," said Vaper.

***

Juan, Derek and Dolly finally arrived at the Millennium Pigeon, only for it still to be surrounded by Orme Troopers. The trio hid behind a pillar.

"How are we going to get on board now?" whispered Derek.

"We'll need to wait until some strange twist of fate distracts the Orme Troopers from watching over it," said Juan.

Then, by some strange twist of fate, the troopers left the ship and headed over to a window to get a ringside seat of the Len v Vaper smackdown. The ship was free to board.

"Quick!" called Juan, "To the Batmobile!" The trio rushed over to the gangway where Arty-Farty and Sheepy-3-0 had already arrived. But as they headed to the ship, events at the window caught Derek's eye. He stopped in his path to the ship and froze.

He watched in horror as Len gave him a knowing smile and then held his telescopic garden handle close to him. In one swift movement, Vaper lashed out with his telescopic garden handle and vanquished Len.

All that was left was Len's brown jacket and a puff of steam. The sort of puff that you get when you take a packet of Uncle Ben's rice out of the microwave.

CHAPTER NINE

"Noooooooooooooooooooooooooooooooooooooooooo oo!" cried Derek.

"Shuttup mun," said Juan but it was too late. The Orme Troopers spun around, and noticing the party about to board the Pigeon, started letting off rounds from their blasters.

Juan and Chico dashed up the gantry to get the engines started and the kettle on. Arty-Farty and Sheepy-3-0 followed but Derek was still in shock at the demise of Len. He was still stood frozen to the spot.

"Get in the ship, dickhead!" called Dolly. She grabbed Derek by the collar and dragged him up the gantry.

The Orme Troopers gave chase, blasting their guns but after a while, they sort of gave up because they were rubbish. As the Pigeon finally lifted from the hangar floor and turned for the blackness of space, Juan strapped his seatbelt on and prepared for a quick getaway.

"That old bastard had better had switched off the tractor beam before he snuffed it," he said, flicking a few buttons and turning Classic FM on.

In the co-pilot's seat, Chico kept an eye on the monitors in front of him and every second that passed, he was convinced that the beam was down. He turned to Juan and gave him a thumbs up with his llama thumb-type thing.

Juan slammed the throttle forward and in a flash, the Pigeon was out of sight of the Debt Star. Watching this from one of the observation platforms aboard the Debt Star stood Vaper and Muff Larkin.

"So you've put a tracking device on this thing have you?"

"Yes," said Vaper, taking a toke on his ciggie, "The fools will lead us directly to their base."

"You'd better be right," said Muff Larkin.

***

The Millennium Pigeon was way out of danger and halfway across the country. But aboard the ship was a very sad sheep. Derek sat at a table and sulked.

"Chin up," said Dolly. "He'd had a good innings."

"That's not the point," replied Derek. "He was a good man."

"I'm sorry for your loss."

"He was a kind man, an honest man."

"Stiff upper lip, eh Derek?"

"He was also an important part of this mission. I'm devastated."

"Like I said, chin up eh?"

"He worked hard."

"So did bloody my washing machine before it bit the dust Derek; now will you stop your whinging please? Jeez."

Dolly stood up and headed to the cockpit where Juan was sat alone. She wanted to speak to someone who didn't have a face half a mile long.

"You ok?" she asked.

Juan was gazing aimlessly out into space. "Yeah, I guess. Just thinking of what I'm going to spend my reward on when I get back."

"Reward? Is that all you're interested in? Your bloody reward?"

"Hey. I'm just a reckless smuggler with a sarcastic wit; I'm also a very practical guy and consider myself a materialist. But do you know what? These adventures have evoked my compassion, a trait I didn't know I possessed."

"Is that all true?" asked Dolly.

Juan turned to her and said:

"I think so. I just read it on Wikipedia so I'm guessing it's true."

Before long, the Millennium Pigeon was nearing Yakult 4 where the rebels had their secret base. The Pigeon swooped low over the jungle-like jungle and touched down on one of their launch pads.

Little did they know that the Debt Star was moving into orbit around their moon, readying itself to implement monthly wheelie bin collections in an instant. In fact, the town was already in its crosshairs. Now it was just a matter of time.

***

In a briefing room down on Yakult 4, General Madonna was stood in front of a very large screen. He was a noble-looking fellow with a big bushy beard and he had a 70s jump suit on. In front of him sat the entire rebel fighter squadron who were awaiting instructions on their next mission. It was an important mission, one that would make or break the rebellion.

General Madonna thumped on the table in front of him and the room fell to a hush.

"Now. We are all in a bit of tight spot. We know that the Debt Star is on its way here to destroy us by implementing monthly wheelie bin collections. You have a very important mission to achieve today and it won't be easy."

He pressed a button and on the screen popped up blueprint plans of the Debt Star.

"These here are the plans that we managed to extract out of the arse of a dog. You can clearly see that the Debt Star is capable of fighting off large scale invasions. Our only hope is that we are small and insignificant and so they won't expecting us."

Another diagram popped up on the screen.

"This here is the exhaust pipe. Your mission is to fly your ships to this exhaust pipe and to ram a banana in it. You'll only have one banana each because some greedy bastard ate the rest of them."

A voice called out.

"That's impossible. That hole is no bigger than 3 inches across. I couldn't even get my..."

"Are you a mouse or a sheep?" growled the General.

"I can do it," said Derek to the sheep next to him. "Having seen off lots of Orme Troopers, I'm now a cocky little shit."

The sheep next to him looked bemused. For years he'd been flying these machines and saving the Universe and then all of a sudden, this twat turns up and thinks he's going to take care of it all.

"I bid you good luck," said the General, before shutting the screen off and ushering everyone out of the room.

***

Down at the hangars, Juan was packing up his reward aboard the Pigeon. Derek strutted over.

"I see. So you're just leaving us then?"

"Looks like it," replied Juan, passing another suitcase of used notes to Chico.

"I thought you were my friend. We've been through a lot together."

Juan put one arm on Derek's shoulder. "Don't be a knobhead all your life, mate. There's a good lad." He gently patted Derek on the cheek.

"Fffffffffffffffffine," said and trotted off in a huff.

***

Derek was finally strapped into his fighter ship. In his helmet, he could hear the chitter chatter of his squadron over the radio. One pilot was moaning that his seat wasn't comfy and another was complaining that his heating wasn't working. On Derek's back seat was Arty who wanted to come along for the ride.

Derek pulled down the sun visor on his helmet and pulled back on his control stick. The fighter lifted gently from its pad and Derek carefully manoeuvred his ship around in its axis.

"Clear to takeoff," came the announcement through his helmet and Derek pushed forward on the throttle and back on the stick. His ship responded well and headed up and out of the hangar to join the line of ships that were headed over the jungle and up to the Debt Star.

He pressed a few buttons but the next thing he knew, he was listening to the voice of Len Konami.

"Derek. The Morse will be with you. Forever and ever. Amen."

Derek shook his head. He'd often hear voices in his head, usually telling him to attack people for no reason or burning someone's barn down.

"Ten minutes until target," came the voice on

the headset. It was his wing commander.

"Roger that," said Derek with an air of importance. The mission was on.

The column of fighters made its way towards the Debt Star that hung in the sky over Yakult 4. The pilots made their last-minute checks as they took aim for their target.

Eventually, the fighters loomed in on the Debt Star. It was a huge construction, built entirely at the tax payers' expense of course.

"Accelerate to attack speed," announced the Commander. The group of ships fired up their afterburners and peeling off one by one, they headed down into the trench where the exhaust port lay.

Peow! Peow!

The Debt Star's main guns let loose a torrent of laser blasts as the fighters dipped down into the trench. There were laser blasts all over the place.

Peow! Peow!

"Red One?"

"What?"

"Are you there?"

"Err. Yeah."

"Good. Aim for the exhaust pipe."

"Yes, sir. Banana at the ready."

Red One sped up to attack speed, narrowly skimming the bottom of the trench and the guns that were trying to blast it out of the sky.

"I'm on target," said Red One. Derek was following close behind when he noticed a Clark's Pie fighter dipping down and latching on to the tail.

"Red One. You have a Pie Fighter on your tail."

"I'm pulling up!" called Red One.

"Stay on it!" barked the Wing Commander

"STAY ON IT!"

Derek tried to pick the Pie Fighter off with a few blasts but he was a bit shit and missed it entirely.

"He's closing in on you!" screamed Derek.

"Stop putting me off, mun! I want to pull up."

"Stay on it!" came the Commander again.

The target came into range of Red One's radar and he squeezed the trigger.

"Banana away!" he called out, pulling back hard on the control stick and pulling his fighter clear out of the trench. Derek watched as the Pie Fighter pulled up with him. But the banana was way off and Derek had to yank hard to the right to avoid crashing into the wayward yellow crescent-shaped fruit.

"He's missed!" called Derek.

"Doom and bloody gloom," said Red One. With his banana gone, all Red One could do now was provide firing cover for another bombing run.

"I'm going in," said Red Two. He swung his fighter down into the trench that Red One had just run and lifted the safety cover on his trigger.

"I'm 30 seconds away from target," said Red Two. He was running in at full pelt and his engines were screaming.

"I'll cover you," said Derek and veered his craft down in after him.

"Twenty seconds," said Red Two.

"Stay on it," said the Commander.

"Ten seconds."

"Stay on it."

"Banana away."

The radio fell silent as the entire fleet awaited the outcome. The radio eventually fizzed back into life.

"Nah," said Derek "Missed that too. Jeez. What's the matter with you all?" He pulled his ship up and around but as he did so, he picked up two Pie Fighters who had just joined the action.

"Well you have a go then, chopsy," ordered the Commander.

"No problem," said Derek confidently. "It'll be like Bugger's Canyon back home." He reeled his ship up and over and then sped out away from the exhaust pipe.

"Where's he going?" asked Red Two.

"He's preparing for an attack run," said the Commander.

Once he'd reached the start of the trench, Derek pulled hard on the control stick and flew the fighter back down to rooftop level, skimming the surface of the Debt Star. He pulled down his heads-up display and flicked the safety switch off the trigger. The two Pie fighters followed hot on his heels and they were swiftly joined by none other than Garth Vaper in his Pie Fighter himself.

"Get that ship," barked Vaper and the trio followed Derek down into the trench.

"Twenty seconds," said Derek.

Vaper lined up Derek a peach and placed his finger on the trigger, ready to blast him out of the sky.

But a sudden explosion next to his ship sent him spinning out of the trench and into the darkness of space.

It was Juan. He'd come back!

"Aw. Thanks hun. I knew you'd come back," yelled Derek triumphantly.

"Just hit the frigging exhaust and get out of there so we can all go home. This story's been dragging on long enough now," cried Juan.

But Derek suddenly heard a voice in his head.

"Use the Morse, Derek, use the Morse." It was Len. Again.

"Jeez Len. Can you just stick a cork in it now mun? You're beginning to get on my tits."

Derek lined up the exhaust pipe in his crosshairs and squeezed on the trigger.

Nothing.

Then, in what seemed like seconds later, his nuclear banana shot off and down into the exhaust like shit off a shovel.

"It's a hit! It's a hit!" he cried, pulling back on the control stick as hard as he could. He pushed his throttle forward as far as it would go. He had to get out before the whole thing went up.

He didn't look back. Within seconds he felt the heat and force of an explosion behind him, lurching him forward in his seat..

Down on Yakult 4, the rebels looked up into the sky. Unfolding before their eyes was the biggest explosion they'd ever seen. It was like the explosion of erm…the Death Star.

The crowds cheered wildly as Derek and the remaining fighters headed for home for a cup of tea and some Malted Milks.

CHAPTER TEN

The main hall at the rebel base was lined with lots of extras that we haven't mentioned in the story so far. There was a big stage at the front of the hall and on it stood Princess Dolly, looking half tidy.

At the other end, two large doors opened and without saying a word, Derek, Juan and Chico walked slowly up the aisle together towards the Princess.

It was a bit like a wedding but with lots of people with helmets on.

The trio walked up and looked at each other and once they arrived at the stage, they all looked at each other. Without saying a word.

Then Dolly gave them some medals and everyone sort of smiled at each other. Without saying a word.

And then Derek and Juan stood there like dicks while everyone clapped and that's the end.

THE END

Also by Derek the Weathersheep
Available from Amazon

ABOUT THE AUTHOR

Derek The Weathersheep lives on a Rex Honey's Farm high in the Brecon Beacons, South Wales.

From his high vantage point, Derek can cast his sheep's eye across the whole of South Wales, and forecast the South Walian population about forthcoming
weather events.

He first caught the meteorological bug when he was just a lamb. He was the first sheep to correctly forecast the great snows of 2006, when he ran to Farmer Honey's house, woke him from his slumber, bleated for a bit, and then led Farmer Honey to the rest of the sheep who were about to be cut off from the farm by the drifts. 48 sheep were rescued that night. Farmer Honey rewarded him by presenting him with the Freedom of Honey Farm.

Derek's girlfriend, Dolly (not to be confused with the famous cloned one- they just look alike) is the best looking ewe on the field, and constantly draws attention from male sheep and sometimes even other female sheep. Juan the LoveSheep, a Spanish import, brought by Farmer Honey, to increase virility in the flock, constantly tries to woo Dolly, much to Derek's dismay and amusement.

Printed in Great Britain
by Amazon